1. Bert Loper 1908 Inscription
Navajo Canyon
W. L. Rusho, photographer
Bureau of Reclamation Collection
photo no. P557-420-3627 (1958)

2. Bert Loper Plaque
Red Canyon
Gus Scott, photographer
photo no. M26 (1954)

3. Loper, Frazier, Kelly Inscriptions
At the base of Sentinel Rock
J. H. Enright, photographer
Bureau of Reclamation Collection
photo no. P557-420-776 (1957)

4. T. Williams 1885 Inscription
Mouth of the Escalante River
Gus Scott, photographer
photo no. A50 (1955)

5. Norm Nevills Inscriptions
Narrow Canyon
W. L. Rusho, photographer
Bureau of Reclamation Collection
photo no. P557-420-8448 (1958)

6. A. J. Tadje 1914 Inscription
Mouth of the Escalante River
Gus Scott, photographer
photo no. A49 (1955)

7. Bernheimer 1922 Inscription
In Redbud Pass
David Breternitz, photographer
photo no. 2 (1957)

8. 9. & 10.
J. K. Hillers, F. S. Dellenbaugh, &
Clem Powell 1872 Inscriptions
Music Temple
Lloyd Pierson, photographer
photo nos. 29, 30, 5 (1958)

11. Bishop 1872 Inscription
Music Temple
Margaret Eiseman, photographer
photo no. 116-21-58 (1958)

12. Crossing of the Fathers Plaque
Erected 1938
Mouth of Padre Creek
A. E. Turner, photographer
Bureau of Reclamation Collection
photo no. P557-420-9869 (1959)

13. Eagle rock carving
Below Hole in the Rock
Katie Lee, photographer
photo no. 67ss (1958)

14. Galloway Inscription
Galloway-Outlaw Cave
A. E. Turner, photographer
Bureau of Reclamation
photo no. P557-420-3557 (1959)

15. Dudy Thomas, R. W. Sprang &
Pard 1950 Inscription
Above Mouth of Rock Creek
Gus Scott, photographer
photo no. B80 (1956)

16. W. H. Buch Inscription
Mystery Canyon
Katie Lee, photographer
photo no. My508pb (1959)

17. H. P. Blake Inscription
Mystery Canyon
Katie Lee, photographer
photo no. My507pb (1959)

18. John Wetherill 1921 Inscription
West Canyon Creek
Katie Lee, photographer
photo no. WC732pb (1956)

19. Lee Ferry Fort-Trading Post
Lees Ferry
Robert Webber, photographer
photo no. 242 (1956)
This sign was taken down as it was quite
inaccurate. The building was built in 1874
by Jacob Hamblin and the St George
Stake as Lees Ferry Trading Post.

the Colorado River through

GLEN CANYON

BEFORE LAKE POWELL

HISTORIC PHOTO JOURNAL 1872 TO 1964

Eleanor Inskip

Editor

Inskip Ink
Moab, Utah
1995

Published by
Inskip Ink ☯ more than ink on paper
Moab, Utah
and
Glen Canyon Natural History Association
Page, Arizona

Printed by
Pyramid Printing, Inc. Grand Junction, Colorado
on 105 lb. Patina Matte Text in Berkeley Oldstyle type
Photo Restoration
Amy Nuernberg, Toby Gadd and Kitty Anderson Nicholason
Design and Typography
Kim Lemons
and with the loving attention of
Stuart Thompson, Marc Terrien, Tim Hebbard and Owen O'Fallon

Copyright 1995
ISBN 0-9648078-1-5 silk
ISBN 0-9648078-0-7 paper

Library of Congress Catalog Card Number 95-79089
First Edition
1500S/8500P

FRONT COVER PHOTO
Aerial view east-southeast over Reflection Canyon and the confluence of the Colorado and San Juan Rivers.
This photo was taken six months after the lake began to fill. The water had risen 100 feet.
Lake Powell buoy number 56.5
William C. Bradley, *photographer*
photo file number GC-1
photo date June 1963

BACK COVER PHOTO
Redbud trees up Little Arch Canyon
Lake Powell buoy number 45
Walter Maeyers Edwards, *photographer*
photo file National Geographic Society
Glen Canyon Collection
photo file number LP-R74F8
photo date 1962

The photographs and quotations throughout this book are credited as they appear and listed on pages 90-93.

CONTENTS

INTRODUCTION

"Glen Canyon"

"Ne'er saw I, never felt, a calm so deep!
The river glideth at his own sweet will:
Dear God! The very canyon seems asleep;
And all that mighty gorge is lying still!"

ADAPTED BY ROBERT BREWSTER STANTON, 1889
FROM WILLIAM WORDSWORTH'S
"Composed Upon Westminster Bridge"
Robert Brewster Stanton, Down the Colorado
Dwight Smith, Editor, 1965

The Colorado River flowed through Glen Canyon for thousands of years before John Wesley Powell's 1871-72 expedition first photographed its beauty. Long before, Native Americans lived in this special place. They left their structures and rock art in Glen Canyon before their story was lost under today's Lake Powell. Lost, too, are the places chronicled by Powell, Robert B. Stanton, C. Gregory Crampton, and other explorers, surveyors, and adventurers who rowed the river before the flood gates on Glen Canyon Dam closed in 1963. Lake Powell drowned Glen Canyon, but we will not forget it.

Glen Canyon was a desert garden. Water seeped from springs in the sandstone walls, ran down the side canyons cascading into pools, from which it quietly flowed onward. It was soft and lush. Cottonwood and Redbud trees, Maidenhair ferns, and a medley of flowers grew in alcoves up the side canyons and along the river. Back in the 30s residents grew grapes and watermelon; one had a fig tree. Great Blue Heron nested in the Cottonwoods lining the river banks.

Glen Canyon was tranquil until a thunderstorm arrived, changing it into a tempestuous, threatening river. Winds could bring a boat to a standstill or send it spinning. A sudden downpour could flood the canyon with rushing water. Six- foot high sand waves, appeared suddenly, rolling upstream before disappearing with a loud roar. River runners would hole up in caves and wait out the fast-moving storms, watching the raw power of Nature's forces and waterfalls spilling over the steep canyon walls.

It is clear from reviewing the literature on Glen Canyon that the light was distinctive. Writers tried to explain: Was it the water seeping out of the nooks and crannies?

The vegetation's green cast? The dryness of the air? The earth's rich hues?

All saw it and were moved by the vision. Glen Canyon was a unique place.

This book is as much a visual history as a tribute to Glen Canyon's sinuous and scenic path. After departing from North Wash near the mouth of the Dirty Devil River, the reader moves downstream toward Lees Ferry—much like the river runners whose adventures provide the book's material. The nearest Lake Powell buoy number identifies each photograph, allowing you to compare today's lake with history's canyon.

Beware
The buoys move with changes in Lake Powell.
You may have to do your own exploring to find just the right angle to see into the past.

ACKNOWLEDGMENTS

I was captivated by the beauty of the landscape and enticed by the river in 1985 when Joseph Antos brought his beautiful Glen Canyon Odyssey slide show to Moab, Utah. I wanted to see more of the canyon hidden under Lake Powell, so my research began. The encouragement of Tammy Morton, former director of the Glen Canyon Natural History Association, and support from the Board of Trustees and the staff at Glen Canyon National Recreation Area, launched my own canyon adventure.

My journey led me to museums, archives, and private collections across the country. I wore little white gloves and sat in antiseptic rooms full of priceless, fragile, photographic prints and negatives. I plunged into poorly-lit basements to exhume dusty boxes holding family albums and treasures. I talked on the phone, wrote letters and went to meetings. I found beautiful pictures, fascinating stories and new friends. One hundred and one photographs were selected from over 6,000 images, and there are 6,000 more I haven't seen. The excerpts taken from journals, letters, and other writings to accompany the pictures reflect my reverence for this unequaled place.

Mary Fredericksen, Joan Nevills Staveley and Gary Ladd were very helpful, providing me with names of people who might have photographs of Glen Canyon before Lake Powell, and looking over my work when I needed feedback.

A conversation with David Brower led me to the National Geographic Society's archives and the Walter Maeyers Edwards (Toppy) collection. I shared my idea with Roy Webb at the University of Utah's Marriott Library and when he later received a collection of photographs from David Gaskill, Roy put us together. David's albums on Glen Canyon took him more than 25 years to gather and organize and have been very helpful in compiling this book. He can read topographic maps and pinpoint a canyon wall with superb accuracy. Katie Lee, Glen Canyon Momma, has been my guiding light throughout this endeavor. Katie loves this canyon with a passion you will be able to experience when you read her book, All My Rivers are Gone (a-book-in-progress).

Bego Gerhart loaned his superb library, and Don Briggs shared his work on the Colorado River. Edie Wilson supplied me with a home in Flagstaff, my base while searching the files at Northern Arizona University, Cline Library and the Museum of Northern Arizona. Dick Sprang, Kent Frost, Margaret Eiseman, Gary Topping, W. L. Rusho, Charles Eggert, Katharine Bartlett, Dick Negri, Ed Dobson, Stan Jones, Bruce Roberts and Dave Breternitz have all shared their memories and knowledge. Technical assistance, editing, proofing and hand holding have been given cheerfully by Duncan Mackie, Michaelene Pendleton, Lee Bennett, Terby Barnes and Christine Calnan.

And each photographer and author must be blessed for the gift of recording Glen Canyon for us.

Thank you all,

Eleanor Inskip, Editor

FOR FURTHER STUDY

Ghosts of Glen Canyon
Crampton & Rusho, Cricket Press 1994

The Colorado River Survey
Robert B. Stanton, Howe Brothers 1987

Lee's Ferry, Desert River Crossing
Rusho & Crampton, Cricket Press 1992

Hole in the Rock
David E. Miller, Utah History Atlas 1984

A Story that Stands Like a Dam
Russell Martin, Henry Holt 1991

Glen Canyon Natural History Association
Lake Powell Boating Guide
Netoff, Ladd, Lamb, Wood & Holland 1989

Rainbow Trails,
Early-Day Adventures in Rainbow Bridge Country
James E. Babbitt 1990

Out of Print — but worth the search
The Place No One Knew
Eliot Porter, Sierra Club Books 1963

"The 1871 [John Wesley Powell] river party had cached one of the boats, the Cañonita, at the mouth of the Dirty Devil River, which marks the head of Glen Canyon. The plan was to take a pack train overland, retrieve the boat, float leisurely through Glen Canyon (there were few serious rapids between the Dirty Devil and Lees Ferry), and take photographs. Powell recognized its spectacular and haunting beauty and wanted to add a Glen Canyon series to the photographic and stereographic collection.

"The trip would bring the boat to Lees Ferry, where the other boats were cached, in time for the planned second leg of the river trip through Marble and Grand Canyons.

"The Cañonita was recovered, caulked, and painted.

"On June 26, 1872 Hillers, Fennemore, Dellenbaugh, and William D. Johnson, Jr., set off through 'Mound' and 'Monument' canyons (the two were subsequently grouped together as 'Glen Canyon' by Powell)."

DON D. FOWLER
The Western Photographs
of John K. Hillers,
Myself in the Water
1989

James Fennemore, photographer
photo files
• National Archives no. 57-PS-778
• Northern Arizona University no. 268-11
• U.S. Geologic Survey no. P10Hist79
• Arizona Historical Society no. 405-35

buoy no. 139

photo date (1872)

NORTH WASH

downstream from the Dirty Devil River

Left to right: W. D. Johnson, Jr. • Frederick S. Dellenbaugh • John K. Hillers

Josef Muench, photographer
photo no. B-6608 (1949)

buoy no. 139

HITE FERRY

"The white man's history of settlement in Glen Canyon began in September, 1883, when Cass Hite, who had been prospecting in the Navajo Mountain country, arrived in company with the Navajo Chief Hoskininni."

C. GREGORY CRAMPTON
Ghosts of Glen Canyon 1994

"There was a dirt-covered rock landing built out from shore, not far, and a pair of heavy cables strung across the river to the western bank. The ferry itself was on the far side where Arth Chaffin, the ferryman, lived in a big house concealed by cottonwoods.

"We rang the bell, as instructed by a signboard...After a while a man appeared among the trees on the opposite shore, stepped

aboard his ferry and started the engine, engaged the winch. The strange craft moved across the river's flow toward us, pulling itself along the sagging cable. It was not a boat. It appeared to be a homemade barge. Whatever it was, it worked, came snug against the landing.

"I drove my pickup aboard, we shook hands with Arth Chaffin and off we went, across the golden Colorado toward that undiscovered West on the other side."

Ferry operated 1946-64

EDWARD ABBEY
"How it Was"
Beyond the Wall, Essays From the Outside
1984

Gus Scott, photographer
photo no. Y33 (1953)

buoy no. 123

BERT LOPER CABIN

"At the age of 79 on July 8, 1949, Bert Loper died running his last rapid in Marble Canyon. He was rowing his hand-made boat on a pleasure trip with fellow boatmen Don Harris, Jack Brennan and Harry Aleson.

"Bert Loper was born July 31, 1869, in Missouri, the day John Wesley Powell camped at the mouth of the San Juan River in Glen Canyon. He lived in this cabin and on the river.

"According to his stone inscription at the base of Sentinel Rock, Loper completed fourteen trips through Glen Canyon.

"In January, 1908 he rowed and towed his boat 150 miles upstream from Lees Ferry to his home in Red Canyon. He married Rachael Jameson in 1916 and they honeymooned on California Bar just below Forgotten Canyon in Glen Canyon.

"Bert Loper lived the river life as a boatbuilder, boatmen, professional guide, placer gold prospector, and adventure photographer. His contemporaries honored him as 'the Grand Old Man of the Colorado River'."

JOHN WEISHEIT
Rivers, manuscript
1994

Joseph Antos, photographer
photo no. 14 (1955)

buoy no. 109-110

TAPESTRY WALL

"The Garden Wall, one of the most imposing cliffs of Glen Canyon, is now known as Tapestry Wall." 1889 trip

Robert B. Stanton, *The Colorado River Survey*
Editors Smith & Crampton 1987

"Some night lie at the mouth of a rock-carved amphitheater two or three times the size of anything you've been in. Look up the thousand foot wall to the billion stars and listen to the murmuring of the river still carving deeper the slot of canyon you're in. Think of nothing but what you see and feel and hear and smell.

"What a campsite we had picked!...beyond us, the river made a lazy curve to the left and there the canyon wall rose straight up a thousand feet. For a mile and a half this cliff followed the river before the wall fell back again. The face of the cliff was stained with long, black streamers from the water which cascaded over the rim in wet weather. It was an imposing sight, a gigantic backdrop a motionless hanging tapestry..."

Charles Eggert
"Forbidden Passage"
Sierra Club Bulletin
1958

Gus Scott, photographer
photo no. B18 (1958)

buoy no. 106

FORGOTTEN CANYON ENTRANCE
view from Smith Fork across the river

"The geology here has changed from the Wingate-Chinle-Shinarump formations to Navajo sandstone, with the uppermost part of the Kayenta formation only slightly above the river. Navajo sandstone erodes into arches, caves and shelters. Springs are abundant; game was plentiful in the green glens (for which the canyon is named); high rock terraces are capped by Pleistocene gravels-lithic industry materials; alluvial flats and sandbars are relatively free of talus. The area represents a type of topography generally hospitable to a hunting-farming people."

GENE FIELD FOSTER
Glen Canyon Archaeology, manuscript
Museum of Northern Arizona
1958

"Some time after 1922 a party of river runners* discovered that this canyon, a major Glen Canyon tributary, had been omitted from the U.S. Geological Survey's river map published that year. On the spot the party promptly named it 'Forgotten Canyon'."

C. GREGORY CRAMPTON
Ghosts of Glen Canyon
1994

* "...the party was Dudy Thomas, Harry Aleson, and Dick Sprang. We formed a partnership to explore and record our findings in Glen in 1952. We spent six weeks on this journey.

"Dudy had suggested the name a year earlier. Using aerial photographs, Dudy and I determined the unmapped canyon at Mile 92 was big and about six miles long.

"We three spent three days exploring Forgotten Canyon to its end. We found a fine cliff dwelling we named Three Warrior Ruin after the pictographs on the wall above it. The ruin is now called Defiance House.

Philip Hyde, photographer
photo no. K2-Glen-13 (1962)

buoy no. 106

IN FORGOTTEN CANYON

"Two additional members of our party that may surprise you:

Pard, my splendidly level-headed shepherd dog—in the tradition of Ed Mesken's dog—and Micky, Dudy's supremely tough, gray and white, short-haired tomcat, who was built like a buffalo, had the heart of a lion, and walked the canyons, wading water, with a tiger's stride, utterly fearless, militant, shrewd, never a problem, always keeping up, and thoroughly at home loving to doze in Anasazi ruins. We called him our Moki Cat."

DICK SPRANG
Letter
1995

Ellsworth L. Kolb, photographer
photo file Northern Arizona University, Cline Library
Emery Kolb Collection no. 568-2324 (1911)

buoy no. 106

1911 SMITH FORK CANYON PETROGLYPH PANEL

"Note the mountain sheep on the arrow. The figures near the center may represent a dance somewhat similar to the masked dances of the Hopi. The large figures on the left, we are told, represent a stone last on which they wove a sandal. The spiral indicates water.

"The quiet waters of Glen Canyon were quite a rest after the torrents above. We found here many evidences of ancient Indians, who had reached the river through side canyons. We found several ruined cliff dwellings with broken pottery and arrow heads scattered about."

ELLSWORTH L. KOLB
"Experiences in the Grand Canyon"
National Geographic Magazine
AUGUST, 1914

Gus Scott photographer
photo no. M49 (1954)

buoy no. 106

1954 SMITH FORK CANYON PETROGLYPH PANEL

"What a story these cliffs could tell! What a romance they could narrate of various tribes, as distinct from each other as the nations of Europe, crowding each other; and at the last of this inoffensive race, coming from the far south, it may be; driven from pillar to post making their last stand in this desert land; to perish of pestilence, or to be almost exterminated by the blood-thirsty tribes that surrounded them—then again, when the tide changed, and a new type of invader travelled from the east, pushing ever to the west, conquering all before them!

ELLSWORTH L. KOLB
Through the Grand Canyon from Wyoming to Mexico
1915

"Moqui Canyon with its beautiful glens was one of the finest;

"the splendor of 180 degree turns, a carpet of green vegetation and flowering plants dripping off the walls of the shaded alcoves and the beaver dams.

"Moqui Canyon was exquisite.

"We deposit our bed rolls and equipment on a dusty bench as the crimson light lingers on the red cliffs—till night envelopes the canyon.

"Beneath a heaven of countless glimmering stars, we bed down for the night, in tune with the faint sounds of the river's waves and ripples dancing with starlight.

"In this solitary place of haunting beauty, we discover the peace and tranquility so often sought, but rarely attained."

JOSEPH ANTOS
Glen Canyon Odyssey
slide show, video
1960

Gus Scott, photographer
photo no. B22 (1958)

buoy no. 99

MOQUI CANYON
at the mouth

Katie Lee, photographer
photo no. H211pb (1955)

buoy no. 93

HALLS CROSSING
floating past

"We have a cool, pleasant ride today, through this part of the canyon. The walls are steadily increasing in altitude, the curves are gentle, and often the river sweeps by an arc of vertical wall, smooth and unbroken, and then by a curve that is variegated by royal arches, mossy alcoves, deep beautiful glens, and painted grottos."

JOHN WESLEY POWELL
Explorations of the Colorado River of the West and Its Tributaries 1869, 1870, 1871, 1872 and *Cañons of the Colorado*
PUBLISHED 1875 AND 1895 RESPECTIVELY

Walter Maeyers Edwards, photographer
photo file National Geographic Society
Glen Canyon Collection no. LP-R57F1 (1962)

buoy no. 93

JUST BELOW HALLS CROSSING

Great Blue Heron Rookery, right bank

"I don't know when the harmony of the canyon began to dawn on me. Everything fit. The willows hanging over the water, the banks of young shoots running parallel to the waters edge in strips as if planted there by hand instead of a receding tide. The heron roost where leaves and branches were splotched white with years of birdshit.

"The way sand stone walls curved gently down, or stabbed into the water's edge, the immense talus slopes tumbling into the river, acting as buttresses for the varnished cliffs rising hundreds of feet to cobalt sky."

KATIE LEE
Journal 1957
All My Rivers Are Gone
a-book-in-progress
1995

Margaret Eiseman, photographer
photo no. 110-27-53 (1953)

buoy no. 89

APPROACHING LAKE CANYON

"Typical of the larger glens was Lake Canyon, up which we rowed a short distance to make camp.

"When the moon cleared the opposite wall of the canyon, it gleamed through a tracery of tamarisk that nodded in the night sky and lulled the watcher through drowsiness into deep cool sleep.

"In the still small hours of early morning, I was awakened by the loveliest sound imaginable—a low liquid bird-call that flowed through the dark like a benediction."

R. B. McGrew
"An Artist on the Colorado"
Desert Magazine
March, 1961

Lloyd Pierson, photographer
photo no. 27 (1958)

buoy no. 89

UP LAKE CANYON

"The tributaries of Glen Canyon are a unique natural museum exhibiting examples of erosion found nowhere else in the world. The walls of the canyon as a whole are like worm-eaten wood, riddled with tunnels on an enormous scale. The smooth bores of their unroofed, twisting holes converge on the common river channel.

"Most of them are quite short, no more than a mile in length, the shortest snaking back only two or three turns before ending abruptly in a circular chamber surrounding a pool into which a trickle may descend through a sculptured channel."

ELIOT PORTER
The Place No One Knew
1963

Gus Scott, photographer
photo no. B-33 (1956)

buoy no. 89

LAKE CANYON
Anasazi Indian Ruin

"There were thirty-six Anasazi sites in the five miles we walked up Lake Canyon."

SIERRA CLUB
Glen Canyon, slide show, movie, video 1964

"The University of Utah archaeologists on the Glen Canyon Salvage Project called this 'Wasp House,' but Dick Sprang and Harry Aleson called it 'the perfect Moki house,' for its undeteriorated state of preservation as well as the elaborate decorative stone and fingerprint work in the mortar.

"Lake Canyon was named for a huge natural lake dammed by the outwash of two converging side canyons several miles upcanyon.

The dam washed out in 1915. The Mormon Hole-in-the-Rock road crossed the dam. Mormon cattleman and historian Albert R. Lyman, who lived there as a small boy with his dad, related weird stories of a sea monster that lived in the lake!"

GARY TOPPING
Letter
1995

Walter Maeyers Edwards, photographer
photo file National Geographic Society
Glen Canyon Collection no. LP-R56F10 (1962)

buoy no. 83.5

UP ANNIES CANYON

"...walked up a little unnamed canyon. We had no sooner entered...when we found a cool spring gushing from a ledge. Of course we stood under it and cooled off and drank our fill...up the canyon...the passage is very narrow and crooked, with extremely high smooth walls. For a mile it twists and turns. Then three side canyons angle in and the passage widens slightly...below the junction of the three canyons, on the west wall, is the coldest spring I have ever felt.

"Since this canyon is unnamed, I recommend as a name Ann's Canyon. Something should be named in honor of one whose good sportsmanship is always evident, and nothing could be more like the refreshing qualities of her presence than the cool waters of our little spring tucked up there, where few people have ever bothered it. I will call it Ann's Canyon henceforward, and if someday I have a magic lamp that could make the name permanent, I will rub the daylights out of it."

named for Ann Rosner, 1940 trip

BARRY GOLDWATER
Delightful Journey Down the Green & Colorado Rivers
1970

"Later a party taken down by Mexican Hat Expeditions had a lady named Annie with them. She especially liked this canyon, so without knowing we named it Annie also."

KATIE LEE
Letter 1995

"Down all these tributaries pour intermittent floods burdened with sand, each grain a chisel able to liberate imprisoned grains from the ancient walls. The streams batter the canyonsides, tearing away all loose material and gouging out deep troughs.

"The narrowness of some canyons—their sides may be hundreds of feet high and less than six feet apart at the bottom—is dramatic evidence of the rapidity of erosion. A few evidently started as tight meanders in the surface rock, in which fast corrosion deepened the channels into wide passages beneath interlocking walls.

"At the sharpest bends the pounding waters have scooped out deep caves, the girdling walls of which envelop an opposite rounded peninsula of rock. These gigantic structures are like loosely articulated elements of an immobile ball and socket joint."

ELIOT PORTER
The Place No One Knew
1963

Edwin E. Larson, photographer
photo no. 15 (1962)

buoy no. 78

STARTING UP ICEBERG CANYON
formerly Wilson Canyon

Walter Maeyers Edwards, photographer
photo file National Geographic Society
Glen Canyon Collection no. LP-R2F26 (1962)

buoy no. 77

OVER THE RINCON
Navajo Mountain behind

"A word about the Rincon. It is a goose neck representing an ancient flood bed of the Colorado River before it had burrowed down some 600 feet more. In its center is a rock island having two sets of rock masses on top like decaying, ill-cared-for teeth...

The diameter of the Rincon is fully 2 miles and is an unbelievably striking phenomenon."

CHARLES L. BERNHEIMER
Field Notes
JUNE 7, 1929

"Rincon is a Spanish word meaning inside corner, angle or nook. Geologists use it to describe an abandoned meander, dry river bed. A long time ago the Colorado River ate through the walls that were in its way leaving the corner high and dry.

"We called this canyon the land of Fantastic Rocks, as it was filled with rocks that had been shaped and carved and hollowed out by eons of flowing water and sand. There were shapes almost incomprehensible and more than enough fuel for the imagination. Water is powerful stuff."

JOSEPH ANTOS
Glen Canyon Odyssey, slide show, video
1960

"Exploring here was fun. We could play hide and seek and make up all sorts of stories. Once upon a time I was a princess...and then a sorceress with just the right scenery from which the prince or sorcerer would appear. Other times we would just wander in awe of the variety of form.

"After a day of riding the quiet river or long hikes into the recesses of mysterious side canyons, we would curl our toes into the soft, cool, white sand and identify forms etched on the opposite cliffs by moonlight and shadows. We loved to remember the words of Shakespeare: 'how sweet the moonlight sleeps upon this bank. Here will we sit and let the sound of music reach our ears. Soft stillness and the night become the touches of sweet harmony.'"

MARGARET EISEMAN
Letter
1995

Margaret Eiseman, photographer
photo no. 111-35-52 (1952)

buoy no. 77

INSIDE THE RINCON

Eliot Porter, photographer
photo file Amon Carter Museum
Eliot Porter Collection no. P1990.70.8360.1 (EK 61-570) (1961)

buoy no. 75

LONGS CANYON

Sunrise, Moon Reflection in Pool, Navajo Creek

"It is reflection that imparts magic to the waters of the Glen Canyon and its tributaries. Every pool and rill, every sheet of flowing water, every wet rock and seep— these mirror with enameled luster the world about. In narrow chasms streams of melted gems flow over purple sand past banks of verdant willow. Small puddles, like shining eyes, fuse the colors of pink rocks and cerulean sky, and wet ripples of mud may do the same thing. Flood and drouth, heat and cold, life and death alter the finer details incessantly, but they leave unchanged the grand plan and the enchanting quality of the Colorado's masterwork."

ELIOT PORTER
The Place No One Knew
1963

Philip Hyde, photographer
photo no. K-Glen-44D (1962)

buoy no. 68

THE MOUTH OF THE ESCALANTE RIVER

"And so they continued down the river. 'To those who have passed through the perils of Cataract Canyon and the real rapids there, the tiny riffles of Glen Canyon would be a joke,' Birney thought. 'To us—utterly inexperienced watermen—the rapids of Glen Canyon seem quite serious. We stop and study them all.'

"Unfortunately, their study seems to have produced little understanding, for they still ran everything the wrong way.

"...Much more serious, though, was a near disaster at the mouth of the Escalante River which, swollen by sudden rainstorms, was creating tricky waves and a large eddy below its mouth. Hughes broke an oar, but Shoemaker

plied a paddle and got the first boat across. Birney had a rougher time, getting caught in the eddy, shipping buckets of water, and in spite of portaging what seemed to be the worst of the rapid, finding he was still in jeopardy of a series of sand waves—temporary swells created by a false bottom of silt precipitating from saturated water."

1932 trip

GARY TOPPING
"Kelly's Glen Canyon Ventures"
Utah Historical Quarterly
SPRING, 1987

"Gregory Natural Bridge spanned (127 feet) Fifty-mile Creek near its confluence with the Escalante River.

"Cowboys saw it first, and a U.S. Geological Survey mapping crew came in 1921.

"In July, 1940, Norman Nevills and a boating party in Glen Canyon walked to the bridge.

"Although other names were suggested, 'discovery' should be credited to Herbert E. Gregory, Geologist."

C. GREGORY CRAMPTON
Ghosts of Glen Canyon
1994

Margaret Eiseman, photographer
photo no. 112-18-56 (1956)

buoy no. 68
7 miles up the Escalante
& 1 mile up Fiftymile Canyon

GREGORY NATURAL BRIDGE
in Fiftymile Canyon, a tributary canyon of the Escalante River

"The trail was Clear Creek itself a stream that could make you look twice at the country it flowed through, at the colors it watered and revealed.

"Everywhere you looked you knew what a setting meant to a place. And in the Cathedral, whether you looked up at evening or in the morning at this miracle of color and design, or whether you looked at the gardens by the altar or the stream that flowed from the nave, you knew what this place meant..."

DAVID BROWER
Time and River Flowing
1964

Philip Hyde, photographer
photo no. K-Glen-73D (1964)

buoy no. 68
& 2.5 miles up the Escalante

CATHEDRAL IN THE DESERT
1.5 miles up Clear Creek Canyon, a tributary of the Escalante River

CATHEDRAL
IN THE
DESERT

"Then we rounded a final corner, and I caught my breath!

"What a fitting climax to this mysterious world of beauty.

"It was as if this were the end toward which all other wonders had been pointing.

"And even more, the prayers for sunshine had been answered...

"A shaft of light shone through a narrow cleft high above the grotto and formed a wedge upon the softly carpeted floor.

"In this place, I thought, no attitude of mind or heart would be possible except one of worship."

FRANK GRIFFEN JR.
Audubon Magazine
FEBRUARY 1966

Walter Maeyers Edwards
photographer

photo file
National Geographic Society
National Park Collection
photo nos.
NP-R24F10
NP-R25F12
(1964)

buoy no. 68
2.5 miles up the Escalante River
& 1.5 miles up Clear Creek Canyon

"I had been pondering the incredible fortitude of the missionary pioneers who had passed that way in 1880...

"Due to over-optimism and perhaps bad judgment, 250 men, women and children, with 83 wagons and many cattle, found themselves committed, with retreat blocked by the first snow of winter, to taking a short cut across some of the roughest country in the west, and to crossing the Colorado at a seemingly impossible place.

"This was where the largest fault in Glen Canyon, now known as Hole-in-the-Rock, split the cliff 1000 feet above and ¾ mile back from the river.

"In six weeks of superhuman toil they blasted an opening through the 'Hole,' built a wagon road down to the water's edge, assembled a ferry raft, and hewed a road up the face of the 250-foot sandstone cliff wall behind our campsite.

continued

Gus Scott, photographer
photo no. Y99 (1953)

buoy no. 66

HOLE IN THE ROCK

from the top of the trail looking across the river

Walter Maeyers Edwards, photographer
photo file National Geographic Society
Glen Canyon Collection no. LP-R15F9 (1962)

buoy no. 66

HOLE IN THE ROCK

from across the river looking at the trail

"The first third of the perilous descent was an angle of 45 degrees, over rock that became slicker and more treacherous with every wagon that went down. They actually drove them all down, with oxen or horses hitched to the front, and as many men as could find a footing hauling back behind. Miraculously, not a wagon was lost.

"When they were all safely across and up the other side, they still had 150 miles of road building over almost impassable country ahead of them. They finally ground to a halt 10 weeks later at what today is the little settlement of Bluff, Utah, on the San Juan River, so exhausted that they decided to settle there, rather than stagger an additional 18 miles to Montezuma, their intended destination. There were no casualties, and three babies were born enroute."

WALTER EDWARDS
Last Look at Glen Canyon, manuscript
NATIONAL GEOGRAPHIC SOCIETY, 1962

Margaret Eiseman, photographer
photo no. 113-21-59 (1959)

buoy no. 65

PUMPKIN ROCK

"Here we are at play again. Sandy Nevills' legs are sticking out of the pumpkin's mouth.

"We didn't just play in Glen Canyon, its singular beauty introduced us to the world of geology, archeology, ethnology and people who spend their lives studying these disciplines.

"We learned to live in complete isolation from most of society's material props and to bask in the serenity of that primeval nature that places one in the time frame of earth history.

"Glen Canyon was a superb teacher."

MARGARET EISEMAN
Letter
1995

Katie Lee, photographer
photo no. 69ss (1959)

buoy no. 57

SAN JUAN RIVER

"We had a rapid shallow river again the following day, October 5th, but the water was not so widely spread out and there were fewer delays. The walls were of orange sandstone, strangely cut up by narrow side canyons some not more than twenty feet wide and twisting back for a quarter of a mile where they expanded into huge amphitheaters, domed and cave-like. Alcoves filled with trees and shrubs also opened from the river, and numerous springs were noted along the cliffs.

"Twelve miles below our camp we passed a stream coming in on the left through a canyon about one thousand feet deep, similar to that of the Colorado. This was the San Juan, now shallow and some eight rods wide."

1871-72 trip

FREDERICK S. DELLENBAUGH
A Canyon Voyage
1908

L.C.B. McCullough, photographer
photo file Northern Arizona University, Cline Library
Georgie Clark Collection: L.C.B. McCullough no. PH92.12.1734 (1961)

buoy no. 55.5

BASKET MAKER CAVE

looking downstream at Hidden Passage, right bank

"Our first camp in Glen Canyon, just below the junction [San Juan River] is almost unimaginably beautiful—a sandstone ledge below two arched caves, with clean cliffs soaring up behind and a long green sandbar across the river.

"Just below us is the masked entrance of Hidden Passage Canyon, which at sunup glows softly red, its outthrust masking wall throwing a strong shadow against the cliff."

1947 trip

WALLACE STEGNER
"San Juan and Glen Canyon"
The Sound of Mountain Water 1969

Margaret Eiseman, photographer
photo no. 115-29-59 (1959)

buoy no. 55.5

HIDDEN PASSAGE

the canyon entrance

"If the shadow that reveals the passage isn't there — if you came upon it [Hidden Passage] in bright morning sunlight, or late afternoon light, or on a cloudy day, you'll miss it most likely."

KATIE LEE
All My Rivers Are Gone
a-book-in-progress
1995

"Hidden Passage, a canyon whose entrance from any viewpoint is lost in a sweep of solid sandstone.

"Set like a stage between two monolithic walls, it threads its way back and forth through successive backdrops as if through a scenery loft."

BRUCE BERGER
"There Was a River"
Mountain Gazette
1975

"All things hidden lead us on and on.

"The root and end of man are secret things,

"But in this rocky heart of solitude

"The fearful, deep, primeval silence brings

"A kind of answer to our WITHER? WHENCE?

"A whisper that can almost tell us WHY."

CID RICKETTS SUMNER
Traveler in the Wilderness
1957

"Hidden Passage was like a ballet in stone."

C. GREGORY CRAMPTON
Ghosts of Glen Canyon
1994

Gus Scott, photographer
photo no. M96 (1954)

buoy no. 55.5

IN HIDDEN PASSAGE

Bruce Berger, photographer
photo no. GC-75.8-62 (1962)

buoy no. 55

MUSIC TEMPLE BAR
just above mouth of Music Temple, looking downstream

"...the whole one hundred and forty-nine miles of Glen Canyon are simply charming; altogether delightful. One can paddle along in any sort of craft, can leave the river in many places, and in general enjoy himself. I have been over the stretch twice, once at low water and again at high, so I speak from abundant experience."

FREDERICK S. DELLENBAUGH
The Romance of the Colorado River, The Story of its Discovery in 1540 with an Account of the Later Explorations and with Special Reference to the Voyages of Powell through the Line of the Great Canyons
1902

Margaret Eiseman, photographer
photo no. 116-9-58 (1958)

buoy no. 55

ENTERING MUSIC TEMPLE

"We find a little grove of box-elder and cottonwood trees; and, turning to the right, we find ourselves in a vast chamber... At the upper end there is a clear, deep pool of water, bordered with verdure.

"Standing by the side of this, we can see the grove at the entrance. The chamber is more than two hundred feet high, five hundred feet long, and two hundred feet wide. Through the ceiling, and on through the rocks for a thousand feet above, there is a narrow, winding skylight; and this is all carved out by a little stream, which only runs during the few showers that fall now and then in this arid country...Here we bring our camp. When 'Old Shady' sings us a song at night, we are pleased to find that this hollow in the rock is filled with sweet sounds. It was doubtless made for an academy of music by its storm born architect; so we name it Music Temple."

JOHN WESLEY POWELL
Explorations of the Colorado River of the West and Its Tributaries 1869, 1870, 1871, 1872 and *Cañons of the Colorado*
PUBLISHED 1875 AND 1895, RESPECTIVELY

Walter Maeyers Edwards, photographer
photo file National Geographic Society
Glen Canyon Collection no. LP-R18F8 (1962)

buoy no. 55

IN MUSIC TEMPLE

"A song could be heard from beneath that dome to the river, nearly half a mile away. A nostalgic spot, so full of whispers of the past, so lovely—the pool, the stone estrade, the bank of ferns and columbine backing the pool, hanging baskets of them overhead clinging to a seep, and the sandstone spire twisting mysteriously out of sight way up above, from where there poured a crystal ribbon of water that dropped its musical notes into the pool.

"I sang in Music Temple every year for ten years—in all that time I never heard anyone shout."

KATIE LEE
All My Rivers Are Gone
a-book-in-progress
1995

"While the sounds of music were echoing off the high vaulted walls, I noticed that a shaft of sunlight from high above was resting on the center of the pool. Suddenly, I stopped singing and gazed in amazement at the pool. An unexpected gust of wind swirling through the cavern had raised a four foot water spout in the center of the pool. There it stood for a few seconds twirling and dancing, spotlighted by the golden shaft of sunlight in the dim mystical cavern."

LARRY R. STUCKI
Glen Canyon, manuscript
1962

"You could stand in the center and hum a one-second note and 11 seconds later it would still be resonating."

G.C. "BLACK GEORGE" SIMMONS
New Orleans Times Picayune
OCTOBER 4, 1987

Margaret Eiseman, photographer
photo no. 117-12-59 (1959)

buoy no. 52

ANASAZI CANYON FORMERLY MYSTERY CANYON
coming off the river

"Mystery [Anasazi] Canyon...Another stupendous declivity in the side of the main canyon...Immense expanses of smooth red rock from the waters edge to the top for at least 1000' and in many places wide blackish purple stripes ran from top to bottom giving the appearance of a wide striped satin curtain...Redbud, juniper, willow, box elder and yucca growing in profusion all the way up and the colors were quite indescribable, all the shades of green imaginable with the delicate yellowish cream of the yucca set against the background of red Navajo sandstone making a continuous picture of peaceful beauty—both awe inspiring and breath taking. The feeling of being so completely isolated from civilization was never so marked as it was here."

ANDREW CHAMBERLAIN
"From Hat to Head of Marble in Six Days"
Journal
1948

Philip Hyde, photographer
photo no. K-Glen-10D (1962)

buoy no. 52

ANASAZI CANYON

walking up

"Of all the phenomena of the side canyons, it is the light, even in the farthest depths of the narrowest canyon, that evokes the ultimate in awe. In somber, rocky caverns of purple and ocher stone into which the sun rarely strikes, shallow pools glitter brassily from sunlit cliffs high overhead.

"Wherever there is a damp cleft, maidenhair fern and scarlet lobelia and white columbine grow. Their drooping leaves turn a dusky cyan-green in the blue shadows, creating a subdued almost funereal atmosphere."

ELIOT PORTER
The Place No One Knew
1963

Dave Evans, photographer
photo file Look Magazine (1950)

buoy no. 52

ANASAZI CANYON POOL

"Six girls steep in a sun bath at the Colorado's Mystery Canyon"

left to right

Martha Moody • Lee Moi Chu • Becky Barnes • Irene Hettinga • Georgia White [Clark] • Irish McCalla

"Shooting a movie in the West's man-killing canyon country makes strong women out of an attractive and hard-working set of starlets. Along with smart cafes, screen tests, lavish parties and weekly paychecks, a movie starlet's life sooner or later leads to an 'on location' job. For the half-dozen young things from Hollywood involved in Capital Enterprise's forthcoming River Goddesses, the location was the Colorado River canyon country."

"Six Girls Against the Colorado"
Look Magazine
MAY 1951

"On one occasion a movie company hired me to help make a movie called 'Six Girls Against the Colorado.' All of the girls were under eighteen so they asked me to play chaperone as well as run the boats."

GEORGIE [WHITE] CLARK AND DUANE NEWCOMB
Georgie Clark, Thirty Years of River Running
1975

This 1950 trip was arranged by Mexican Hat Expeditions.

Robert Gaskill, photographer
photo no. GC-32-58 (1958)

buoy no. 51

ABOVE THE MOUTH OF OAK CREEK CANYON
Navajo Mountain behind

"We soon arrived at a pretty rapid with a clear chute. It was not large, but it was the only real one we had seen in this canyon and dashed through it with pleasure.

"Just below we halted to look admiringly up at Navajo Mountain which now loomed beside us on the left to an altitude of 10,388 feet above sea level or more than 7,100 feet above our position, as was later determined.

"The Major [John Wesley Powell] contemplated stopping long enough for a climb to the top but on appealing to Andy

for information as the state of the supplies he found we were near the last crust and he decided that we had better pull on as steadily as possible towards El Vado."

FREDERICK S. DELLENBAUGH
*A Canyon Voyage, The Narrative of the
Second Powell Expedition down the
Green-Colorado River from Wyoming,
and the Explorations on Land
in the Years 1871 and 1872*
1908

unknown photographer
photo file Utah Historical Society
Aleson Collection, C-187, Box 4, no. 22 (pre 1963)

buoy no. 51

TWILIGHT CANYON

six-fingered petroglyph near mouth of the canyon

"Twilight: 500 ft. walls, v/tight, no sky...lg. cave and petrographs at entrance, lg. open face cave, perfect camp site...many beaver."

JUNE CHAMBERLAIN
Journal
1947

"Petroglyph Workshop Twilight Canyon.

The site is about 400 yards upstream from the river, and 50 feet northeast from the creek. The ground at the base of the cliff is covered with flakes, broken blades, etc.

"On a separate boulder facing the river are several spiral or curvilinear patterns.

On the cliff next to this rock are large concentrations of petroglyphs."

GENE FIELD FOSTER
Glen Canyon Archaeology, manuscript
Museum of Northern Arizona
1958

Christy G. Turner II, photographer
photo file Museum of Northern Arizona
Glen Canyon Collection, no. 3 (1958)

buoy no. 49

MOUTH OF AZTEC CREEK

"Camp at mouth of Aztec: here was absolute peace and quiet...Mourning Doves, swallows, bats...

"The surrounding cliffs reflected beautifully on the still water of the lagoon, the reflection as clear as the originals."

HELEN KENDALL
Journal
1948

Walter Maeyers Edwards, photographer
photo file National Geographic Society
Glen Canyon Collection no. LP-R68F7 (1962)

buoy no. 49

FORBIDDING CANYON

on the trail to Rainbow Bridge

"And now, Great God of the River and of the Universe, we offer
this tribute to you in gratitude for the safe passage you have so far afforded us. Amen"

NORMAN NEVILLS' PRAYER
as reported by
Andrew Chamberlain, 1948 Journal
Blue Mountain Shadows, Webb
1993

Remo Lavagnino, photographer
photo no. GC-1-63 (1963)

buoy no. 49

BRIDGE CANYON

"In the side canyons, along the narrow water courses where deep pools are carved in rock and the flow is clear and constant, lives a small plump, gray bird with stumpy tail, the water ouzel. A favorite haunt is the narrows in Bridge Canyon...He makes his living, in the flowing streams and cascades of high country and canyons of the west...he never departs far from them...When first encountered he will probably be bobbing on a stone in midstream, and...may suddenly plunge into the foaming water. Over his somber dry gray suit he instantly slips a resplendent jacket of shiny silver bubbles and walks about on the bottom picking up aquatic larvae here and there showing as little concern as he would on dry land. In a moment he pops out again...He is apparently pleased with his mode of life, bursting into song most unexpectedly after emerging from one of his underwater foraging expeditions. He sings his ebullient, varied song through the year for no other assignable reason than the sheer joy of doing so..."

ELIOT PORTER
The Place No One Knew
1963

"At the confluence of Bridge and Aztec Creek lived a family of little green turtles – you could hold in the palm of your hand."

KATIE LEE
All My Rivers Are Gone
a-book-in-progress
1995

"Makes one feel almost as if this were Fairyland...I can't imagine anything more perfect than walking up Bridge Canyon."

DORIS NEVILLS
"Woman Conqueror of the Colorado"
Grand Junction Daily Sentinel
1941

Stuart M. Young, photographer
photo file Northern Arizona University, Cline Library
Special Collections & Archives no. 643-1-123 (1909)

buoy no. 49

RAINBOW BRIDGE

the first photograph

The first expedition *transcribed by Barry Goldwater from the Rainbow Bridge Register, in 1940*

"Noschowbigay then promised to guide Mr. Wetherill and Professor Cummings to the arch...in June, 1909. Professor Cummings and his party of students were working in Sagie Canyon waiting for Mr. Wetherill...Mr. Wetherill came to the Sagie for the trip, but brought letters stating that Mr. W. B. Douglass, as inspector of surveys for the U.S. Government, was at Bluff endeavoring to have the permit of the Utah party cancelled, and that he would be at Oljato in three days on his way to Navajo Mountain, also in quest of the big arch of which he had learned the winter before from Mrs. Wetherill. In courtesy to a representative of the U.S. Government... Mr. Cummings and Mr. Wetherill turned back to Oljato to meet Mr. Douglass and join forces...On reaching Paiute Canyon, Noschowbigay was away on the mesa with his sheep, but his father sent for him and he took the party beyond the slick rocks late that night. He then led the Utah party to the arch, altho Mr. Douglass had urged both before and after his arrival that there was no use of going on and that they should give up the quest. Noschowbigay...from Paiute Canyon, was the official guide of the party and the only man [in the party] who knew the location of the arch...Professor Cummings is the first white man to have seen this great natural wonder and Mr. John Wetherill first passed under...These facts can be verified from any one of the several men accompanying the expedition."

BARRY GOLDWATER
Delightful Journey, Down the Green & Colorado Rivers
1970

Stuart M. Young, photographer
photo file Northern Arizona University, Cline Library
Special Collections & Archives no. 643-1-130 (1909)

buoy no. 49

CUMMINGS-DOUGLASS-WETHERILL
1909 RAINBOW BRIDGE EXPEDITION

Photo Members

Back Row-left to right

John English • Dan Perkins • Jack Keenan • Francis Jean Rogerson • Neil M. Judd • Donald Beauregard

Front Row-left to right

Jim Mike • John Wetherill • Byron Cummings • William Boone Douglass • Malcom Cummings

Not in photo

Stuart M. Young • Dougi Begay • Nasja Begay

Joseph Antos, photographer
photo no. GC-11-55 (1955)

buoy no. 49

OVER THE RAINBOW BRIDGE

"On the day of the discovery [August 14, 1909] a few men walked down Bridge and Aztec Creeks to the Colorado River. There they found mining and camping equipment scattered about and what appeared to be some prehistoric structures at the mouth of the canyon. Prospectors working in Glen Canyon and exploring in the Navajo Mountain area were certainly the first whites to see the bridge, but they didn't bother to report the fact, and, of course, the Indians had known of it for centuries. It was the Cummings-Douglass 'discovery' in 1909 that led to the formation of Rainbow Bridge National Monument proclaimed by President Taft in 1910."

C. GREGORY CRAMPTON
Ghosts of Glen Canyon
1994

Katie Lee, photographer
photo no. 113 ss (1959)

buoy no. 47

CASCADE CANYON

"The bedding of the sandstone is so peculiar as to excite wonder and admiration. The cross-bedding is on a scale which for extent and perfection of detail is difficult to exaggerate.

"In places the curved laminae (lines) have uninterrupted sweeps of two hundred to three hundred feet...many cliff faces are decorated by close-set loops and arabesques comparable to the lathe work in steel engravings..."

JULIUS STONE
Canyon Country: The Romance of a Drop of Water and a Grain of Sand
1932

56

Philip Hyde, photographer
photo no. K2 Glen-43 (1962)

buoy no. 45.5

CATHEDRAL CANYON

"In Cathedral Canyon...the floor disappears into a water-filled trough...Swimming through it is a dreamlike adventure. Shivering, we glide along like seals...through still depths into an inscrutable solitude...in a journey reminiscent of Xanadu, 'through caverns measureless to man'.

"A sudden shaft of sun, giving a dimension of reality, penetrates the upper stories through an unseen window. It lights a strip of wall a dazzling yellow and is reflected to our eyes at water level from the thin curved edge where the pool laps the rock in gentle undulations, like golden threads reaching ahead to delineate for a moment the wavering separation of water from stone...Shivering, we retrace our way, glad to emerge at last into the August sun."

ELIOT PORTER
The Place No One Knew 1963

Felix E. Mutschler, photographer
photo no. GC-1-13-62 (1962)

buoy no. 45

DRIFTWOOD CANYON

from the mouth, looking upstream

"One of the peculiar features of this Canyon are (sic) the extensive broad level flats of bottom land in the great bends of the River, in places covered with black willow and scrub oak, which with the red walls of the Canyon, form such pleasing pictures.

"These large flats, by actual measurements – in later years – contain over 15,000 acres of gravel and fine sandy loam, much of which, in by-gone-ages, was cultivated by that long forgotten race that built their homes, their grain-houses or corn cribs, and their extensive system of fortifications, along and on the Canyon walls."

1889-90 trip

ROBERT B. STANTON
Down the Colorado, Robert B. Stanton
Dwight Smith, Editor
1965

"It is my first diary. I have noted the humdrum of our camps, the incidents and adventures...but have given little, very little description of the beautiful grand scenery we have passed through. It would take a Goethe to describe it."

1871-72 trip

W. C. [CLEM] POWELL
Journal, Utah Historical Quarterly
1947-49

W. C. Bradley, photographer
photo no. GC-16-58 (1958)

buoy no. 45

LITTLE ARCH CANYON

from the mouth, looking upstream

"Past these towering monuments, past these mounded billows of orange sandstone, past these oak-set-glens, past these fern-decked alcoves...we glide hour after hour, stopping now and then, as our attention is arrested by some new wonder."

JOHN WESLEY POWELL
Explorations of the Colorado River of the West and Its Tributaries 1869, 1870, 1871, 1872 and *Cañons of the Colorado*
PUBLISHED 1875 AND 1895 RESPECTIVELY

"Little Arch Canyon was short, fern gutted and very narrow...Where the canyon said 'stop' a pool lay rippleless in a bowl of sand. Innocent. But looking up I could feel the rage of storm borne water that sometimes poured from the convoluted labyrinth, now dry. It was through this twisting mystery I wanted to go...

"Walls like rippled blue-grey veils seemed to move with me as I spiraled upward through the slender passage...50 yards and it ended. I leaned against a stone teepee 100 feet tall, its smoke hole revealed pink walls 550 feet more above that.

"No sound but my breathing. Has a human stood here before: I think I'm the first... what a gift! Standing in the twilight bottom of that bowl of stone flooded the senses. Touching the velvet walls gave me the sensation of being in the timeless womb of Mother Earth...

"This is the first holy place I have ever been."

KATIE LEE
All My Rivers Are Gone
a-book-in-progress
1995

Walter Maeyers Edwards, photographer
photo file National Geographic Society
Glen Canyon Collection no. LP-R70F35 (1962)

buoy no. 45

IN LITTLE ARCH CANYON

Katie Lee, photographer
photo nos. BR645pb, BR642pb, BR644pb, 131ss (1955-56)

buoy no. 45

BALANCED ROCK CANYON

"Just when we thought we had seen all the categories and the rest would be permutation, we would stumble onto something like the shelf of balanced rocks. I was familiar with that American classic, Balanced Rock, the boulder dancing on a pin...pride of every state in the West. I was unprepared for an entire shelf of balanced rocks no more than knee-high. Wind had eroded rotten sandstone beneath an assortment of granite, gneiss, and quartzite boulders, compressing the sandstone at their weightiest points and leaving them perched on finely whittled fingers. Some rocks stood on one leg, some on two or three, and sometimes a pebble was lodged, incredibly, between the sandstone peg and the boulder. Oblong, dark, river-polished, ludicrous, these balanced rocks were more like eccentric tea tables."

BRUCE BERGER
There Was A River
1994

Katie Lee, photographer
photo no. F657pb (1957)

buoy no. 44

MOUNTAIN SHEEP CANYON

formerly False Entrance Canyon

"The broad river moves between towering, colorfully striped and textured cliffs, green glens and amphitheaters, bridges and arches, monoliths, slots in the canyon walls which may be eroded joints or cleavage planes, short box canyons or the mouth of major tributary valleys.

"The latter two are characterized by beautiful, endlessly winding, spring-fed and sand-floored valleys, with huge trees and widely varied flowering plants."

GENE FIELD FOSTER
Glen Canyon Archaeology, manuscript
Museum of Northern Arizona
1958

Philip Hyde, photographer
photo no. K-Glen-27D (1962)

buoy no. 40

DANGLING ROPE CANYON

"Dangling rope? Yes there was one. Some river runners* promptly named the canyon when they found a rope dangling down over a 40-foot slope. At the same place there were 19 or 20 pecked steps, possibly of prehistoric origin though they had been enlarged by later users.

"When I visited the site a cottonwood log was standing below the steps making it possible for an agile person to reach the lowest one. Our party did not attempt to climb the trail, given the shallow toe-hold steps and the uncertain condition of the rope. We concluded that the route had been used by a prospecting party during the uranium boom after World War II."

C. GREGORY CRAMPTON
Ghosts of Glen Canyon
1994

Katie Lee, photographer
photo no. 133ss (1956)

buoy no. 40

DANGLING ROPE CANYON

* "On the right about the first turn after entering the canyon there is a makeshift ladder, some moqui's [steps] and a rope dangling from the cliff above – if one wanted to take his life in his hands one could probably get up."

KATIE LEE
Journal 1957
All My Rivers Are Gone
a-book-in-progress
1995

Katie Lee, photographer
photo no. C667pb (1955)

buoy no. 40

CORNERSTONE CANYON

J. Frank Wright in center of photo was the owner of Mexican Hat River Expeditions. Frank was a major source of information on Glen Canyon for the Museum of Northern Arizona's Archaeological Reclamation Salvage work.

"I always found Glen Canyon to be one of my favorite trips. My main interest in running rivers of course, was to experience the rapids. There weren't many on Glen but the scenery more than made up for this.

"Glen Canyon itself was completely isolated and miles and miles from the nearest civilization. During the 1950s there probably weren't more than four or five people in hundreds of square miles of desert."

GEORGIE CLARK AND DUANE NEWCOMB
Georgie Clark, Thirty Years of River Running
1975

Alvin Colville, photographer
photo no. GC-60.3-62 (1962)

buoy no. 39.5

WETHERILL CANYON

from the mouth, looking downstream

"The river still in shadow, picks up color and multiplies it, converting gray stones along its muddy bank into uncut lapis lazuli embedded in molten bronze. Blue highlights thread the dry sand ripples. Day is near and will soon blaze into the canyons depths.

"All the bizarre morning colors fade with the day's advance. Purple banks and blue dunes become common mud and sand. The river becomes muddy green. The rocks turn to brick and clay as the sun climbs above the canyon rim."

ELIOT PORTER
The Place No One Knew
1963

"Our second journey through Glen Canyon, though made in December, was in the weather of early fall.

"The excessive heat of the summer had gone. The nights were cool, but the wildflowers in the lower stretches of the Canyon were still in bloom.

"Though the willows were touched by frost their leaves were still on. The exquisite shade of the first yellow; the light green of the young protected sprouts, mingling with the browns of the dry grasses on the great flats; the bright red of the autumn oak leaves; all seen against the walls of variegated shales, of creamy orange above, then bright vermilion, and below purple and chocolate beds, with, at their foot, hillocks of green and yellow sands all made a color scheme and a picture most pleasing to look upon, worthy of an artist's brush, but which, much to my regret, my camera could not catch."

1889-90 trip

ROBERT BREWSTER STANTON
Down the Colorado, Robert B. Stanton
Dwight Smith, Editor
1965

Christy G. Turner II, photographer
photo file Museum of Northern Arizona
Glen Canyon Collection no. 10 (1959)

buoy no. 39.5

IN WETHERILL CANYON

Katie Lee, photograph
photo no. 138ss (1957)

buoy no. 39

DEEP IN GROTTO CANYON

Katie Lee tried for half an hour to get up, but had to quit because it was too slick

"In less than half a mile it ends, like many others, in a deep pool—above that a twisting purple-pink grotto trickles clear, cold water—all surrounded by forty foot high banks of maiden-hair fern—shimmering emeralds, more alive, even more delicate than those in Little Arch! Still, it isn't at all like Little Arch.

These canyons have different personalities, even though they drain from the same plateau.

The sand and gravel floor of this canyon is flat, its little stream meanders, the big pool holds a bouquet of watercress, sweet but tangy—we browse on it."

KATIE LEE
All My Rivers Are Gone
a-book-in-progress
1995

68

"The vaulting walls closed in, squeezing
ever closer, letting only the faintest
trickle of light ooze from the far sky
while we filed through as phantoms.
Ever twisting and convoluted, the
passage lengthened to a long nave of
staggered piers in the style of late
English gothic. There was no sound but
the thread of our voices, our feet
disturbing the pebbled floor, and the
silence of eras gripped in stone.

"At this compulsory stopping place, the
stone hurtled upward at a mad slant
hundreds of feet, in parallels that nearly
touched. Here it was always either dusk
or night, and if there is consciousness in
stone, this stone was insane."

BRUCE BERGER
There Was a River
1994

Sarah Moench, photographer
photo no. 11 (1961)

buoy no. 38

IN DUNGEON CANYON

Dick Sprang, photographer
photo no. G5-11 (1955)

buoy no. 35

ROCK CREEK

"Archaeological sites were found at every place visited throughout this part of the canyon."

GENE FIELD FOSTER
Glen Canyon Archaeology, manuscript
Museum of Northern Arizona
1958

[The area referenced was between Dangling Rope and the Rock Creek Canyons.]

Katie Lee, photographer
photo no. WC724pb (1956)

buoy no. 28.5

WEST CANYON CREEK

"SHELTER, SHERDS, GLYPHS.

The West Canyon Creek sites were reported by Tad Nichols...
The description below is from conversation and (in quotes)
correspondence.

About .5 mile beyond the petroglyphs is a Navaho [sic] stock
trail, and 'a couple hundred yards upstream from the trail' is the
shelter or...'just a long overhanging wall, no sign of rock
structure, just gently sloping dry dirt floor direct to the stream.

Hand and footholds had been chipped in the rock back to afford
access up to the cave level. Painted drawings on the cliff wall, a
red hand, a couple of white circles. Also, bedrock metates. All
undisturbed.' Bones, sticks and ashes are in evidence on the
floor. The sherds collected are especially interesting: 2 are
unlike any found in Glen Canyon before."

GENE FIELD FOSTER
Glen Canyon Archaeology, manuscript
Museum of Northern Arizona 1958

Sarah Moench, photographer
photo no. 25 (1960)

buoy no. 28.5

UP WEST CANYON CREEK

"Of the three (one multiple) sites in West Canyon, one is definitely Anasazi, one is definitely Navajo, and the other is a multiple-use site probably used for over three hundred years.

"The pecked steps at the mouth would provide an access trail from the mouth to the highlands on the north side or right bank of West Canyon. This would make possible overland travel which was faster and might be preferred by the Anasazi.

"Navajo, with their sheep, would more likely, in this area, come down the creek bed, finding access elsewhere to the Carmel terrace grazing."

NATALIE B. PATTISON AND
LOREN D. POTTER
Prehistoric and Historic Steps and
Trails of Glen Canyon-Lake Powell
1977

"Members of the reconnaissance party [Rainbow Bridge-Monument Valley Expedition] that made the 200-mile passage through the canyons of the San Juan and Colorado report need for thorough biological fieldwork along river courses.

"The area is as outstanding from the point of view of scientific interest as it is scenically.

"Investigations of the past summer have indicated that the archaeological story, when it is more completely worked out, may be one of the most complete and fascinating in the whole Southwest.

"There are many geological problems of utmost importance which demand solution. For the biological field sciences the region presents almost a virgin field.

"For these reasons it is recommended that the work of the Expedition be continued for at least two or three more field sessions."

Respectfully submitted to:
The Secretary of the Interior,
The Commissioner,
Office of Indian Affairs, and
The Director, National Park Service
BY ANSEL FRANKLIN HALL
FEBRUARY 20, 1934

Christy G. Turner, II, photographer
photo file Museum of Northern Arizona
Glen Canyon Collection no. 13 (1958)

buoy no. 28.5

WEST CANYON CREEK

Edwin E. Larson, photographer
photo no. GC-5 (1963)

buoy no. 28

GREGORY BUTTE

"Gregory Butte, a majestic formation...named for geologist Herbert E. Gregory (1869-1952). Among his many scientific publications, Gregory wrote five geological monographs blanketing the entire southern section of the Glen Canyon region; all were published as professional papers by the U.S. Geological Survey between 1915 and 1951.

"In these studies, based on extensive field work, he devoted much space to human history and geographical features often lacking in literature bearing the geological label.

"Gregory's monographs on the Navajo country, the Kaiparowits Plateau, and the San Juan region should be counted among the basic books on the canyon country."

C. GREGORY CRAMPTON
Ghosts of Glen Canyon
1994

Christy G. Turner II, photographer
photo file Museum of Northern Arizona
Glen Canyon Collection no. 15 (1959)

buoy no. 28

SPRING TRAIL CANYON

"Glen Canyon was for delight.

"The river that used to run here cooperated with the scenery by flowing swift and smooth, without a major rapid. Any ordinary boatman could take anyone through it...There was superlative camping anywhere, on sandbars furred with tamarisk and willow, under cliffs that whispered with the sound of flowing water...

"Glen Canyon, once the most serenely beautiful of all the canyons of the Colorado River."

1947 trip

WALLACE STEGNER
The Sound of Mountain Water
1969

Christy G. Turner II, photographer
photo file Museum of Northern Arizona
Glen Canyon Collection no. 8 (1958)

buoy no. 25

MESKEN BAR

"Edward Mesken, colorful Glen Canyon figure, staked out his bar on September, 1889, during the interval between the first and second Stanton trips through Glen Canyon. Since known as Mesken Bar, the placer was on the right bank forty-five miles above Lees Ferry. Stanton was busy these days staking claims and looking to the railroad survey...He refers frequently to the notes made on the first trip through Glen Canyon in late June and July."

1889-90 trip

ROBERT BREWSTER STANTON
*The Colorado River Survey, Robert B. Stanton and the
Denver, Colorado Canyon and Pacific Railroad*
C. Gregory Crampton and Dwight D. Smith Editors, 1987

"On the 19th, we met Edward Mesken, an old trapper and prospector, and his dog, Sport. They had been on the river for nearly five years, though we passed last summer without seeing them. Our night at their camp was at least one bright spot in their lonely lives."

ROBERT BREWSTER STANTON
Down the Colorado, Robert B. Stanton
Dwight Smith, Editor
1965

Katie Lee, photographer
photo no. F749pb (1956)

buoy no. 23

FACE CANYON

camping at the mouth of the canyon

"It doesn't matter; before this voyage is done we will become, as I have witnessed on every river journey yet, one anarchic but reasonably happy family. It seldom fails: there's something about a progress down a river that brings out the best in anyone. Getting bored with your neuroses:

"Drop your analyst—drop him/her like a cold potato—and make tracks for the nearest river.

" 'If there is magic on this planet,' wrote Loren Eiseley, somewhere (I quote from memory), 'it lies in flowing water.' Amen"

EDWARD ABBEY
One Life At a Time
1988

Gus Scott, photographer
photo no. A109 (1955)

buoy no. 22

KANE WASH

view upstream

"As the shore approached, more machinery took shape, and we found the slope covered with a strange growth. We beached and were instantly mobbed by a human cacophony: pink-faced men in straw hats and sunglasses, expressionless Navajos... overweight housewives with squalling children, tall Anglo men with beards, rabble that escaped categories. Cameras clicked in our faces. Had we crossed the Styx? Were these to be our hellmates?

"Natalie managed to outshout them. 'So, who exactly are you?' One of the bearded men replied, 'We're filming the life story of Jesus.'

"As we stared at the slope behind, where the strange growth resolved into plastic olive trees, we learned that George Stevens Productions had selected Kane Creek to film a best-seller called *The Greatest Story Ever Told*, cast of thousands, galaxy of stars.

" 'Here's where we're doing the baptism scene,' the bearded apostle went on, 'you know, when John the Baptist sprinkles water on Jesus' head. This isn't the Colorado. You just ran the Jordan.' "

BRUCE BERGER
There Was a River
1994

Walter Maeyers Edwards, photographer
photo file National Geographic Society
Glen Canyon Collection no. LP-R23F24 (1962)

buoy no. 21

APPROACHING CROSSING OF THE FATHERS

"In the year 1776 Father Escalante, a Spanish priest, made an expedition from Santa Fe to the northwest, crossing the Grand and the Green, and then passing down along the Wasatch Mountains and the southern plateaus, until he reached Rio Virgin. His intention was to cross to the Mission of Monterey: but, from the information received from the Indian, he decided that the route was impracticable. Not wishing to return to Santa Fe over the circuitous route by which he had just traveled, he attempted to go by one more direct, and which led him across the Colorado, at a point known as El Vado de Los Padres.

"From the description which we have read, we are enabled to determine this place. A little stream comes down through a very narrow side canyon from the west. It was down this that he came, and, our boats are lying at the point where the ford crosses."

JOHN WESLEY POWELL
*Explorations of the Colorado River of the West and Its Tributaries
1869, 1870, 1871, 1872* and *Cañons of the Colorado*
PUBLISHED 1875 AND 1895 RESPECTIVELY

Joseph Antos, photographer
photo no. 12 (1955)

buoy no. 21

PADRE CANYON

"The coloring of the Canyon walls is generally red, streaked with black by the weather. The red is not itself brilliant, but the effect of the morning and evening sun shining upon the cliffs, through the peculiar atmosphere of that dry country, produces the most startling effect, till the whole side of the Canyon seems ablaze with scarlet flame. In the late evening, as one is looking up the River at some massive wall that seems, in the shadow, to be black rather than red, suddenly the sunlight streams through a side canyon, and in an instant the whole cliff flashes out in living fire, so bright, so startling, as to be unreal, for it is the color of the sun's rays, not the wall; but the wall is needed to bring the color to your eye, and it stands as if painted in veritable scarlet."

1889-90 trip

ROBERT BREWSTER STANTON
Down the Colorado. Robert Brewster Stanton
DWIGHT SMITH, EDITOR, 1965

Walter Maeyers Edwards, photographer
photo file National Geographic Society
Glen Canyon Collection no. LP-R40F29 (1962)

buoy no. 17

TOWER BUTTE

aerial view above Navajo Creek, north-east toward Navajo Mountain

"Eons of erosion have created a land that from the air looks truly fearsome and forbidding. Distance lends no enchantment to this view.

"Yet later on the ground we discovered Glen Canyon to be a treasure trove of loveliness, whose secret has never been fully told."

WALTER MAEYERS EDWARDS
Last Look at Glen Canyon manuscript
National Geographic Society
1962

"The side canyons are far more meandering at creek level than at their rims and therefore more sinuous than is shown on topographic maps."

GENE FIELD FOSTER
Glen Canyon Archaeology manuscript
Museum of Northern Arizona
1958

L. C. B. McCullough, photographer
photo file Northern Arizona University, Cline Library
Georgie Clark Collection: L.C.B. McCullough
no. PH-92-12-252 (1955)

buoy no. 17

GUNSIGHT BUTTE

"By 1922, the natural beauty of the river canyons was beginning to be appreciated...Dr. John A. Widstoe, enroute to Santa Fe that year to represent Utah in the signing of the Colorado River Compact, toured Glen Canyon in company with a distinguished group of Geological Survey and Reclamation Service officials, to look over the most suitable dam sites. The party, led by E. C. La Rue, entered the river at Hall's Crossing and saw the Hole-in-the-Rock Crossing, Rainbow Bridge, the Crossing of the Fathers...as well as the possible dam sites...Widstoe wrote

'...I quite agree with Major Powell, that it is useless to describe with words or even with pictures the wonders, of surprising magnitude and beauty, that fills the country through which we have passed on this trip'."

C. GREGORY CRAMPTON
Standing Up Country
1964

Gus Scott, photographer
photo no. H132 (1954)

buoy no. 17

WARM CREEK

"On the downstream wall of Warm Creek Canyon, with the aid of Charles Larabee of Kansas City, I placed in the red sandstone above highwater level the following inscription, chiseled and filled with white lead:

ARIZONA
WELCOMES
YOU | UTAH

"We took pictures and were off again. The line marked is probably off the actual state line by one hundred feet or so, but we placed the inscription here for practical purposes."

1940 trip

BARRY GOLDWATER
Delightful Journey Down the Green and Colorado Rivers
1970

David Breternitz, photographer
photo no. 1 (1957)

buoy no. 10

NAVAJO CANYON

"My cousin Ruell Randall, and I just walked away from a family picnic in the Blue [Abajo] Mountains passed Indian Creek then proceeded walking to Hite where we encountered Arth Chaffin. He looked at the raft we had built to float Glen Canyon, and invited us to stay for a week, so's he could make us a boat. We stayed and then set off downriver for adventure in a boat that floated gracefully on the almost clear and extremely low water.

"The San Juan River was dry. We killed a beaver to eat, discovered it tasted like mud, so we used it for catfish bait. Some placer miners invited us to dinner, beef jerky gravy over biscuits. It was wonderful.

"The clear river turned to mud as we approached Navajo Canyon, it was discharging a huge flood and the sand waves were scary but we came through right side up. Our speed was then greatly increased.

"All those miles from Hite to Lees Ferry took us seven days. We arrived home a little over a month from the day we walked away from the picnic. Our families seemed glad to see us."

1939 trip

KENT FROST, ORAL INTERVIEW
1995

"Toward evening we camped at the head of a small rapid near a fine little stream coming in from the left which we named Navajo Creek. The river was about four hundred feet wide with walls on each side of four hundred feet in height.

"The next morning Prof., Cap. and I climbed out for bearings reaching an altitude a mile or so back from the river of 875 feet. Everywhere we discovered broken pottery, fragments of arrow-heads, and other evidences of former Shinumo occupancy. Even granting only a few persons at each possible locality, the canyons of the Colorado and Green must have been the former home of a rather large population."

FREDERICK S. DELLENBAUGH
A Canyon Voyage,
The Narrative of the Second Powell Expedition
down the Green-Colorado River from Wyoming,
and the Explorations on Land,
in the Years 1871 and 1872
1908

David Breternitz, photographer
photo no. 3 (1957)

buoy no. 10

NAVAJO CANYON

"In the afternoon we ran a little rapid and kept on for about six miles making twenty in all from El Vado, when we camped on a heavy talus on the left.

"The following morning, October 18th, we had not gone more than a mile when we came to a singular freak of erosion, a lone sandstone pinnacle on the right, three hundred or four hundred feet high, the river running on one side and a beautiful creek eight feet wide on the other.

"We named these Sentinel Rock and Sentinel Creek and camped there for Beaman to get some photographs."

FREDERICK S. DELLENBAUGH
A Canyon Voyage, The Narrative of the Second Powell Expedition down the Green-Colorado River from Wyoming, and the Explorations on Land in the Years 1871 and 1872
1908

Josef Muench, photographer
photo no. B-419 (1949)

buoy no. 11

SENTINEL ROCK

"A giant monolith of red sandstone guards the entrance of Wahweap Canyon into the Colorado River, Arizona. Passengers on an upstream trip to Rainbow Bridge pause to enjoy the dramatic spot set in the brilliant cliffs. My friend Art Green, took me exploring in the canyons of the Colorado."

JOSEF MUENCH
1949

Katie Lee, photographer
photo no. 77 (1954)

river mile 8

FERRY SWALE

"Weather in the canyon country is not always good. Storms sweep over it from the northwest, the outriggers of disturbances down from the Aleutians, and may last for a week enveloping the canyon in mist and rain.

"More usually, summer's bad weather is local and short-lived. Storms develop over the bordering plateaus, spreading out over the encircling land until darkening thunderheads rumble their warning.

"Down in the canyon, where the cliff-edged sky is narrow, they can surprise you. A white-edged, black cloud rises above the canyon rim, lightning flickers, a crash ricochets down the canyon, and the first drops spatter dark wet circles on the red sandstone. They evaporate quickly from the hot surface but their replacements come fast. A dusty smell pervades the hot air.

continued

"The rain curves into the canyon in gusts, bright points and streaks against dark cliffs. The drops seem to float down but they strike the face hard. The black cloud now possesses the entire opening of sky and a cold wind sweeps through the canyon. Another flash of lightning brightens the obscurity and thunder crashes again, much louder, reverberating from higher terraces, rolling and rumbling up and down the gorge, dying in the cul-de-sacs.

"The rain comes down hard now. The wet cliffs have lost all color, but glisten like mercury from the sheets of water pouring over them. Through the notches and dips in the rim, wherever the walls were streaked, streams pour down.

"Through larger notches torrents spume over, free-falling hundreds of feet with a roar, some white and clean, others brown and murky. The noise of falling water and the rush of the rising creek drown out all but the thunder."

ELIOT PORTER
The Place No One Knew
1963

Katie Lee, photographer
photo no. 78 (1954)

river mile 8

FERRY SWALE

Margaret Eiseman, photographer
photo no. 126-20-53 (1953)

river mile 0

LEES FERRY

"In the canyon itself the days flow through your consciousness as the river flows along its course, without a break and with hardly a ripple to disturb their smoothness. Problems fade from the forefront of your mind. Duration becomes a serene timeless flow without landmarks, without interruptions, without the insistent beckoning of obligations. The river supplies and in a sense supplants the need for a measure of time. The current becomes the time on which you move. Things happen and days pass. They exist simply in a heap of impressions and memories, all different and yet all of one kind. There is no more liberating or healing experience.

"It penetrates to the very core of being, scattering anxieties, untangling knots, re-creating the spirit.

"To put the world, and yourself at the same time, in a valid perspective you must remove yourself from the demands of both. The world's demands fade the faster, but nonetheless surely your own will shrink to acceptable proportions and cannot sally forth to attack you. In the wilderness of Glen Canyon you do not assail yourself.

You glide on into the day unpursued, living, as all good river travelers should, in the present."

ELIOT PORTER
The Place No One Knew
1963

EPILOGUE

"On January 21, 1963 the floodgates closed
and Lake Powell, 'The Jewel of the Colorado'
began its slow ascent.

One by one the sand bars, the river banks,
the hidden oases of the side canyons succumbed.

And with them died all they supported –
the cottonwoods, willows, redbuds and
tamarisk, the beaver and deer and rodents,
the plants, even the insects.

Torn from all that sustained them,
the herons and egrets had nowhere to go.
Ruins, petroglyphs, pictographs, dredges:
history too disappeared.

Mile by mile the water lapped upstream,
leaving Glen Canyon simplified."

BRUCE BERGER
"There Was a River"
Mountain Gazette
1975

PHOTOGRAPHY CREDITS

alphabetical by photographer

© **Joseph Antos**
p.13, no. 14
p.54, no. GC-11-55
p.79, no. 12

© **Bruce Berger**
p.41, no. GC-75.8-62

© **William C. Bradley**
front cover, no. GC-1
p.58, no. GC-16-58

© **Dave Breternitz**
inside front cover, no. 2
p.83 no. 1
p.84 no. 3

© **Alvin Colville**
p.65, no. GC-60.3-62

Walter Maeyers Edwards
© **National Geographic Society**
p.20, no. LP-R57F1
p.24, no. LP-R56F10
p.26, no. LP-R2F26
p.32, no. NP-R24F10
p.33, no. NP-R25F12
p.35, no. LP-R15F9
p.43, no. LP-R18F8
p.50, no. LP-R68F7
p.59, no. LP-R70F35
p.78, no. LP-R23F24
p.80, no. LP-R40F29
back cover, no. LP-R74F8

© **Margaret Eiseman**
inside front cover, no. 116-21-58
p.21, no. 110-27-53
p.27, no. 111-35-52
p.30, no. 112-18-56
p.36, no. 113-21-59
p.39, no. 115-29-59
p.42, no. 116-9-58
p.44, no. 117-12-59
p.88, no. 126-20-53

J. H. Enright
© **Bureau of Reclamation**
inside front cover,
no. P557-420-776

Dave Evans
© **Look Magazine**
p.46

James Fennemore
© **Northern Arizona University**
Cline Library, Special
Collections
p.10, no. 268-11

© **Robert Gaskill**
p.47, no. GC-32-58

© **Philip Hyde**
p.15, no. K2-Glen-13
p.29, no. K-Glen-44D
p.31, no. K-Glen-73D
p.45, no. K-Glen-10D
p.56, no. K2-Glen-43
p.62, no. K-Glen-27D

Ellsworth Kolb
© **Northern Arizona University**
Cline Library, Special
Collections
p.17, no. 568-2324

© **Edwin E. Larson**
p.25, no. 15
p.73, no. GC-5

© **Remo Lavagnino**
p.51, no. GC-1-63

© **Katie Lee**
inside front cover, nos. 67ss,
My507pb, My508pb,
WC732pb
p.19, no. H211pb
p.37, no. 69ss
p.55, no. 113ss
p.60, nos. BR642pb, BR644pb,
BR645pb, 131ss
p.61, no. F657pb
p.63, no. 133ss
p.64, no. C667pb
p.67, no. 138ss
p.70, no. WC724pb
p.76, no. F749pb
p.86, no. 77
p.87, no. 78

PHOTOGRAPHY CREDITS
alphabetical by photographer

© **Sarah Moench**
p.68, no. 11
p.71, no. 25

© **Josef Muench**
p.11, no. B-6608
p.85, no. B-419

L. C. B. McCullough
© **Northern Arizona University
Cline Library, Special
Collections**
p.38, no. PH92-12-1734
p.81, no. PH92-12-252

© **Felix E. Mutschler**
p.57, no. GC-1-13-62

© **Lloyd Pierson**
inside front cover,
nos. 29,30,5
p. 22, no. 27

Eliot Porter
© **Amon Carter Museum**
p.28, no. EK-61-570/
P1990-70.8360.1

W. L. Rusho
© **Bureau of Reclamation**
inside front cover,
no. P557-420-3627
no. P557-420-8448

© **Gus Scott**
inside front cover,
nos. M-26, A50, A49, B80
p.12, no. Y33
p.14, no. B18
p.17, no. M49
p.18, no. B22
p.23, no. B33
p.34, no. Y99
p.40, no. M96
p.77, no. A109
p.82, no. H132

© **Dick Sprang**
p.69, no. G5-11

A. E. Turner
© **Bureau of Reclamation**
inside front cover,
no. P557-420-9869
no. P557-420-3557

Christy G. Turner II
© **Museum of Northern
Arizona**
p.49, no. 3
p.66, no. 10
p.72, no. 13
p.74, no. 15
p.75, no. 8

Unknown Photographer
© **Utah Historical Society
Aleson Collection**
p.48, C-187, Box 4, no. 22

© **Robert Webber**
inside front cover, no. 242

Stuart M. Young
© **Northern Arizona University
Cline Library, Special
Collections**
p.52, no. 643-1-123
p.53, no. 643-1-130

JOURNAL CREDITS
alphabetical by author

Edward Abbey
p.11
"How it Was", *Beyond the Wall, Essays From the Outside*
Henry Holt & Co., 1984

p.76
One Life At a Time, Henry Holt & Co., 1988

Joseph Antos
p.18, p.26
Glen Canyon Odyssey, slide show, video, 1960

Bruce Berger
p.39, Epilogue "There Was a River"
Mountain Gazette, 1975

p.60, p.68, p.77
There Was a River, University of Arizona Press, 1994

Charles L. Bernheimer
p. 26
Field Notes, June 7, 1929
American Museum of Natural History

David Brower
p.31
Time and River Flowing, Sierra Club Books, 1964

Andrew Chamberlain
p.44
"From Hat to Head of Marble in Six Days"
Journal, 1948, Special Collections, University of Utah Libraries

p.50
Norman Nevills' prayer, *Journal,* 1948
Blue Mountain Shadows, Webb, 1993

June Chamberlain
p.48
Journal, 1947, Special Collections, University of Utah Libraries

Georgie Clark and Duane Newcomb
p.46, p.64
Georgie Clark, Thirty Years of River Running
Chronicle Books, 1975

C. Gregory Crampton and W. L. Rusho
p.11, p.15, p.30, p.54, p.62, p.73
Ghosts of Glen Canyon, Publishers Place, 1988
Cricket Press, 1994

C. Gregory Crampton
p.81
Standing Up Country
Alfred A. Knopf & University of Utah Press
& Amon Carter Museum, 1964

Frederick S. Dellenbaugh
p.41
The Romance of the Colorado River, The Story of its Discovery in 1540 with an Account of the Later Explorations and with Special Reference to the Voyages of Powell through the Line of the Great Canyons
G. P. Putnam's Sons, 1902, Rio Grande Press, 1962

p.37, p.47, p.84, p.85
A Canyon Voyage, The Narrative of the Second Powell Expedition down the Green-Colorado River from Wyoming, and the Explorations on Land in the Years 1871 and 1872
Yale University Press, 1908-62
University of Arizona Press, 1984

Walter Maeyers Edwards
p.34-35, p.80
Last Look at Glen Canyon, manuscript
National Geographic Society, 1962

Charles Eggert
p.13
"Forbidden Passage" *Sierra Club Bulletin,* 1958

Margaret Eiseman
p.27, p.36
Letter, 1995

Gene Field Foster
p.14, p.48, p.61, p.69, p.70, p.80
Glen Canyon Archaeology, manuscript
Museum of Northern Arizona, 1958

Don D. Fowler
p.10
The Western Photographs of John K. Hillers, Myself in the Water
Smithsonian Institution Press, 1989

Kent Frost
p.83
Oral Interview, 1995

Barry Goldwater
p.24, p.52, p.82
Delightful Journey Down the Green & Colorado Rivers
Arizona Historical Foundation, 1970

Frank Griffen Jr.
p.32
Audubon Magazine, February 1966

Ansel Franklin Hall
p.72
General Report Rainbow Bridge-Monument Valley Expedition of 1933
University of California Press, 1934

JOURNAL CREDITS

alphabetical by author

Helen Kendall
p.49
Journal, 1948, Special Collections, University of Utah Libraries

Ellsworth L. Kolb
p.17
Through the Grand Canyon from Wyoming to Mexico, MacMillan, 1915

p.16
"Experiences in the Grand Canyon"
National Geographic Magazine, August, 1914

Katie Lee
p.24
Letter, 1995

p.20, p.39, p.43, p.51, p.59, p.63, p.67
Journals, 1953-63, *All My Rivers Are Gone*, a-book-in-progress, 1995

Look Magazine
p.46
"Six Girls Against the Colorado", *Look Magazine*, May 1951

R. B. McGrew
p.21
"An Artist on the Colorado", *Desert Magazine*, March, 1961

Doris Nevills
p.51
"Woman Conqueror of the Colorado"
Grand Junction Daily Sentinel, 1941

Natalie B. Pattison and Loren D. Potter
p.71
Prehistoric and Historic Steps and Trails of Glen Canyon-Lake Powell
Lake Powell Research Project Bulletin, No. 45
National Science Foundation, University of California, 1977

Eliot Porter
p.22, p.25, p.28, p.45, p.51, p.56, p.65, p.86-88
The Place No One Knew, Sierra Club Books, 1963

John Wesley Powell
p.19, p.42, p.58, p.78
Explorations of the Colorado River of the West and Its Tributaries
    1869, 1870, 1871, 1872
US Government Printing Office, 1875 and
Cañons of the Colorado, Scribners, 1895
Parts of both texts can be found in various combinations
    in many books.
Current Publishers are:
    Penguin Books USA, VISTA Books, Dover Publications

W. C. [Clem] Powell
p.57
Journal, 1871-72; *Utah Historical Quarterly*, Vols. 15-17, 1947-49

Sierra Club
p.23
Glen Canyon, slide show, movie, video, 1964

G. C. "Black George" Simmons
p.43
New Orleans Times Picayune, October 4, 1987

Dick Sprang
p.15
Letter, 1995

Robert B. Stanton
p.13, p.75
The Colorado River Survey, Dwight Smith & C. Gregory
Crampton, Editors, Howe Brothers, 1987

p.57, p.66, p.75, p.79
Down the Colorado, Robert B. Stanton
Dwight Smith, Editor, University of Oklahoma Press, 1965

Wallace Stegner
p.38, p.74
"San Juan and Glen Canyon"
The Sound of Mountain Water, Doubleday Publishing, 1969

Julius Stone
p.55
Canyon Country: The Romance of a Drop of Water and a Grain of Sand
G. P. Putnam's Sons, 1932

Larry R. Stucki
p.43
Glen Canyon, manuscript, 1962

Cid Ricketts Sumner
p.40
Traveler in the Wilderness, Harper Collins, 1957

Gary Topping
p.23
Letter, 1995

p.29
"Kelly's Glen Canyon Ventures"
Utah Historical Quarterly, Spring, 1987

John Weisheit
p.12
Rivers, manuscript, 1994

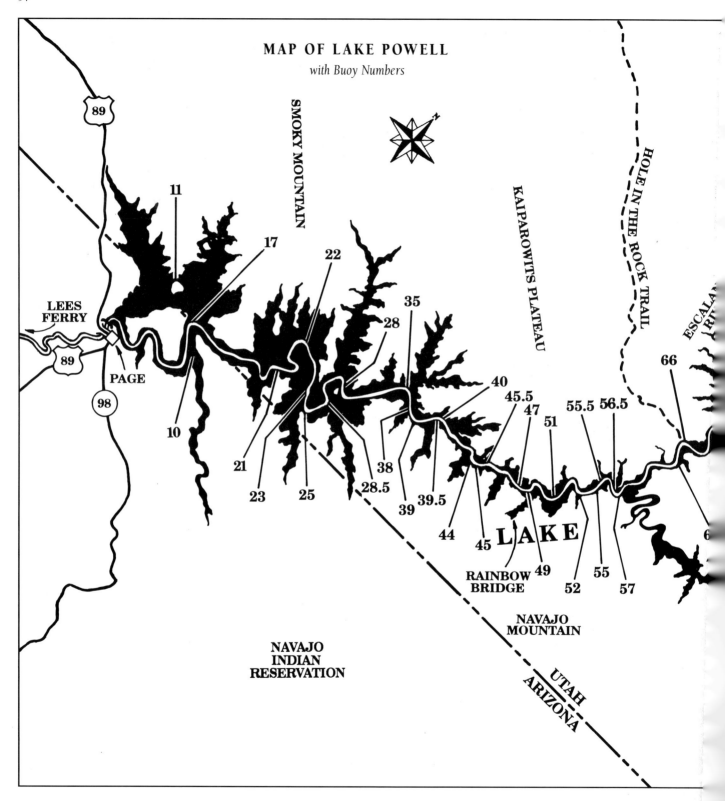

MAP OF LAKE POWELL
with Buoy Numbers